SHOPIFY

A Beginner's Guide With Proven Steps On How To Make Money Online With Shopify Dropshipping Ecommerce

Descrierea CIP a Bibliotecii Naţionale a României
PARKER, GREG

    Shopify. A Beginner's Guide With Proven Steps On How To Make Money Online With Shopify Dropshipping Ecommerce / by Greg Parker. – Bucureşti : My Ebook, 2018
    ISBN 978-606-983-602-6

336
004

SHOPIFY

A BEGINNER'S GUIDE WITH PROVEN STEPS ON HOW TO MAKE MONEY ONLINE WITH SHOPIFY DROPSHIPPING ECOMMERCE

My Ebook Publishing House
Bucharest, 2018

CONTENTS

INTRODUCTION

I want to thank you and congratulate you for buying the book, "Shopify: A Beginner's Guide With Proven Steps On How To Make Money Online With Shopify Dropshipping Ecommerce".

This book contains proven steps and strategies on how to start, grow and succeed in business using Shopify. This book covers tips for small scale and large scale businesses to increase their revenue and build a formidable client base.

Thanks again for purchasing this book, I hope you enjoy it!

This document is geared towards providing exact and reliable information in regards to the topic and issue covered. The publication is sold with the idea that the publisher is not required to render accounting, officially permitted, or otherwise, qualified services. If advice is necessary, legal or professional, a practiced individual in the profession should be ordered.

- From a Declaration of Principles which was accepted and approved equally by a Committee of the American Bar Association and a Committee of Publishers and Associations.

In no way is it legal to reproduce, duplicate, or transmit any part of this document in either electronic means or in printed format. Recording of this publication is strictly prohibited and any storage of this document is not allowed unless with written permission from the publisher. All rights reserved.

The information provided herein is stated to be truthful and consistent, in that any liability, in terms of inattention or otherwise, by any usage or abuse of any policies, processes, or directions contained within is the solitary and utter responsibility of the recipient reader. Under no circumstances will any legal responsibility or blame be held against the publisher for any reparation, damages, or monetary loss due to the information herein, either directly or indirectly.

Respective authors own all copyrights not held by the publisher.

The information herein is offered for informational purposes solely, and is universal as so. The presentation of the information is without contract or any type of guarantee assurance.

The trademarks that are used are without any consent, and the publication of the trademark is without permission or backing by the trademark owner. All trademarks and brands within this book are for clarifying purposes only and are the owned by the owners themselves, not affiliated with this document.

Chapter 1

WHAT IS SHOPIFY?

Advancement in technology has also been marked by a significant increase in online shopping. Consumers are looking for a comfortable and attractive way to meet their needs, and online shopping has made good and services to be just a few clicks away. Meeting this need might just be the opportunity you have been waiting for. Without creating a full ecommerce site you can still have your goods and services displayed over the internet. One way to achieve this is by using the very credible Shopify.

Shopify is an ecommerce website created for entrepreneurs and everyone desiring an online store that will product to be noticed and sold over the internet. Shopify is a highly reputable online shopping center with a lot of users. Some users of this trusted site have made million and thousands of pounds without significant effort. With Shopify, you can track orders, respond to orders, organize your wares, use a customized shop front or the already existing professional design, get access to ready-to-use templates and also get paid using credit cards.

Irrespective of what you are selling be it goods or service, or the size of your business whether big or small, Shopify is a useful tool for your business advancement. Your business can be one of the thousands of business using the secured domain hosting, unlimited bandwidth, and servers with the speed of light and hassle free Shopify provides for their stores.

Shopify is home to any product that is legal to be sold on the internet. You will find products such as e-books, clothes, domestic wares, shoes, musical instruments, edibles and a host of others.

Shopify is also concerned about your offline store and has provided the Shopify's Point of Sale system through you can merge the two stores and therefore manage sales and take inventory as though you have just one store. The Shopify mobile app can be used to manage stores and other activities that pertain to the store.

History of Shopify

Shopify is an e-commerce company whose headquarters is located in Ottawa, Ontario. It also founded an ecommerce platform that goes by the name Shopify for online shops, but it started originally as an online store. Daniel Weinand, Tobias Lütke, Scott Lake founded Shopify in the year 2004, after trying to start an online store which they named SnowDevil for sales of Snowboarding facilities. It was the unsatisfactory experience provided by the then existing ecommerce that led to the building of Shopify. Shopify was initially named "SnowDevil" when it was a store, and it sold snowboards. When it changed to an ecommerce platform its first name "Jaded Pixel."

In 2010 their free mobile app was introduced on the Apple app store allowing shop owners to view their store as well as manage their shops from their mobile devices. In the same year, the Build-A-Business competition was introduced, and participant created businesses with their platform. Cash prizes were given to the winners of the competition and they also gave the opportunity to be mentored by renowned entrepreneurs like Richard Branson and others. In 2012, the net worth of products sold on Shopify had grown to$740 million with about 40,000 stores. It was named "Canada's Smartest Company" by Profit Magazine in 2012 and also Ottawa's fastest growing company.

Chapter 2

HOW TO MAKE MONEY ON SHOPIFY

Ready to make money on Shopify? Then follow the guidelines on how to set up your store and boost your sales given in this book. Remember that anything can be sold on Shopify.

Start up by signing up

Visit Shopify main site (Shopify.com) and click on the link provided to sign up for an account. You will need to enter a functioning email address because you will need to confirm your email. Some other personal information will be required once your account is created such as your name, your product name, your address, your revenue and phone number. After this, you can now choose a store name that suits you. The next step is to sign in with your details, then click the button labelled "create an online store" which will take you to your dashboard to begin the store creating process.

The name provided in the above step will be included in the URL from your store, but this can be changed later. At this point, your Shopify store is fully activated and ready for use.

Making money on Shopify
Getting your products on Shopify

As earlier stated in this book, Shopify products range from physical products.

Products can be added in different ways such as a manual entering of individual products, importing of products from other ecommerce platforms, or a bulk upload from a CSV file. Digital products are added to an app so, you will need to install the app first before adding digital products. For services, you will need an app called "Product Options" to allow you organize your services. Your products can have several variations; these variations can be grouped under specific options. You can also sell different options for your services.

Customize Your StoreFront

From the theme settings editor, you can choose from Shopify's range of themes to optimize the look of your store. There are several theme plans ranging from free to paid plans. Another way to modify your shop design is through the template editor that affects the front end codes (HTML, CSS, and JavaScript), including your personal details, social media links making it easier for visitors to contact you.

The Domain Name

If you your domain name to be different from the regular shopify.com, you can follow the steps in the Shopify online manual or perhaps purchase one if you do not already have one.

Maximizing Profit

Dropshipping is the main idea behind making profit on Shopify. It entails buying goods at a very much reduced rate from countries that sell at cheaper rates like

China. Aliexpress is a good site to consider for dropshipping. Aliexpress provides a list of resalable goods you might want to consider adding to your store. You can add a variety of the desired products to your store.

As a starter, you might not be getting lots of sale for some time, so it is wise for you to choose products with large profit margins that will sustain you while you build your store. Consider products that will sell for much more than they were bought without seeming expensive.

Shipping and Tax rates.

Shopify includes some basic rates for starters. These added costs maybe modified to suit the cost of products. Asides this, tax rates and shipping costs are usually attached to the price of the goods. But if you already included it in the main price, you can indicate that you had already done so.

Order of Payment

Perhaps you are considering how you will be paid for sold products. Shopify has a payment scheme that can accept payment with credit cards without setting up a merchant account. It only functions for shop owners in the USA, UK, and Canada. Other payment processing services such as google Wallet, PayPal, Amazon Payments can also be used to receive payments for transactions done on Shopify.

Reveal your store to the Public

After carrying out the following steps, your store is now fully ready for visitors to have access. Ensure you run several checks on your site before granting public access. Make sure all the sections are functioning well, and everything is in place. Be first to notice malfunctions and mistakes to avoid losing potential customers.

Apart from selling on Shopify, there are several other ways you can make money using Shopify. They are listed below

Be an affiliate on Shopfy: Shopify gives you 200% of the customer's payment for every referral you make. If you have an active blog or large fan base on social media, you might want to consider this.

Partner with Shopify: With knowledge in web development you can build apps and themes for Shopify. A percentage of the amount generated from themes designed by you will be yours. This is another lucrative aspect of Shopify which many people are making lots of money.

Become a Shopify Expert: You can render services to stores on Shopify and get a handsome pay depending on the services your rendered. This is another way to make money on Shopify, but the criteria for this is having an app of your own or a theme in the theme store.

Refer a client to Shopify: Shopify pays you 20% monthly revenue share for every person you get to set up a shop on Shopify. Great! As your client increase sales, your revenue also increases. Like an affiliate marketing program. You can make as much as $5000 monthly from referral.

If selling is not your thing, you may consider one of the options listed above.

Chapter 3

SHOPIFY AND SEO

Creating a Shopify store is not just enough, for you to generate traffic on your site free of advert charges, you must make your site show up in search engines the organic way. Optimizing your Shopify page is very critical to the growth of your business on Shopify. Search Engine Optimization (SEO) takes time; it is a gradual process that will eventually lead to thousands of people visiting your site. As a starter, you need to focus on building the foundation of your business and think little about the stress involved. This chapter will serve as a guide to how you can optimize and improve sales on your Shopify using search engines.

SEO has two parts: the Onsite SEO and the Offsite SEO.

Onsite SEO

Onsite search engine optimization is achieved by choosing the right keywords to rank for and then updating your page to include those keywords in titles, body content, description and every other appropriate place. You also have to ensure that your page has links that point at the relevant page. When using on site SEO, the first thing to do is to look for keywords has a large search volume, which is less competitive and is relevant to your target audience.

Keywords that are frequently searched for are right keywords because they keep bringing out your site each time, the query is sent on a search engine. As much as we want a keyword with many searches, we also want one that is less competitive and will boost our rank when searched for. If you share a keyword with an already established site, the site will rank first before yours. In cases like this, it is better you look for a different keyword, or you would have to wait for a long time to get your site ranking well. Some users are looking for information about your products and may not be looking to buy the products itself. You have to look for keywords that point to the fact that your site is a shopping site. Whatever keyword you decide to choose to make sure it is relevant to your product.

Getting the Right Keyword

Remember that our keywords should have a high search volume, a low difficulty score (the difficulty in reaching the front page of search engines) and must also be relevant to your products. Search volumes vary for different key words are not fixed they vary according to different niches but keywords with search volumes ranging from 1000 – 6000 is good enough, but more preferably around 2000. The difficulty score of a keyword should not exceed thirty-five, the lower it is, the better. A keyword with a difficult score of twenty with a high search volume is best for your site. Each product or a small group of products should have two or three keywords that will be representing the products as a whole. If you sell a variety of products then chose two to three keywords that will be optimizing each of the categories.

Optimizing the Page

After deciding on which set of keywords you are going to be using, the next step involves optimizing your page to use this keyword. This process is divided into three parts

1. Optimizing your homepage for your keywords.

2. Optimizing other pages for your category keywords

3. Setting up links to all of your optimized pages

Optimizing your main page with your primary keywords

For your home page optimization, follow the steps listed below:

1) From your preferences, you can include the top keyword you chose for your site in the homepage title. Just click on Preferences in the Shopify app or page.

2) Ensure that your page Meta description contains relevant and information about your store and products and also including your primary keyword.

3) On your homepage include a heading with a brief content having one or two paragraphs and be sure to add your primary keywords in the page heading a well as the content of the page

4) The "alt" text in your img tag of the images on your homepage should also contain your primary keyword. You can also achieve this by editing the ALT text of a

product image that will be on your home page and also the ALT text on a slideshow or hero image

Optimize other pages on your site for your category keywords

We are also going to ensure that each of our chosen keywords will have some pages or at least one fully optimized page exist on our site for that particular keyword. We want to make sure that for each of our target keywords, we have at least one page on your site that's fully optimized for that keyword. Depending on our choice of a keyword or the best option we may decide to set our pages either as products, pages, blog posts or collections.

For example, if your keywords to be optimized are more general like books, then it best fit into a collection category on Shopify. Following, we would have to create a collection with the name "books" in its title or description, or we edit an existing collection to use the keyword in its keyword. However, for a more specific keyword such as "Hard Cover Exercise Books", you will need to create a product page hat is specific. We can now edit the product page ensuring that the keyword is included in its title and description. Blog posts are created for ranking keywords that are both general and informational. You can write a blog post having the keyword in its title and content. You can use a blog post for keyword showing good potential for optimizing your site.

For optimization of your page, a collection, product, or blog post, the steps stated below are critical to consider and include;

1. The Keyword should be included the title.

2. The Keyword should be part of the body text, content or description or (one appearance at the beginning or within the first two to three sentences of the content and possibly once more for pages containing several paragraphs of text)

3. The keyword should also be in the URL

4. Include one image or more images whose ALT text has the keyword included in its sentence.

5. Embed relevant and appropriate videos such as YouTube videos especially if you run a blog or you deal on product images. Better still, create your customized videos, and then from YouTube upload it on your site.

Internal links to your site

After the optimization of your pages, collections, products, and blog posts with the chosen keywords have been done, the next important step is ensuring that links that connect to those pages are available within your site. Creating a collection without a link to the collection in our navigation tool on the site shows that the site may be of little or no relevance. Google might consider it less important as there are stated links for users to find the page.

It doesn't matter where the link is located in your site, whether in the homepage siite navigation or it's in the footer menu, just ensure that all the optimized pages for your keywords are linked. If you are finding it difficult to include your new collections in your navigation bar without making it look clumsy, then you can consider a random distribution of these collection and product links in your blog post and other pages. For much more important keywords create a Categories menu consisting of the key- word optimized pages. But as much as possible try to include them in your navigation menu.

Site speed optimization

Google usually penalizes sites that take time to load. Ensure that you have done everything it takes to speed up the loading process of your site. You can check the points listed below to be sure if it's just the next thing you should try.

• Limit the amount of Shopify apps that you install as they may add widgets that reduces the loading speed of the site. Certain features accompanying apps, as well as third party scripts, can also slow down your site. From time to time, check for unwanted stuffs on your apps and get rid of them.

• Using high quality images are cool and maybe too large to load quickly. Image compressor apps such as Minifier and ImageOptim can be used to compress and shrink image sizes without stress. The common cause of slow loading of Shopify stores has been attributed to extremely large images. In the absence of image compressor apps, you can also make use of Photoshop or any other image editor to save the image for web or as compressed JPEG file which also reduces the file size as well. For site speed optimization images sizes should not exceed 150kb with a dimension no larger than 1500px.

Mobile optimization

Your site should be responsive which means that it should be cool when viewed from a PC as well as when viewed from mobile devices. If your site does not adapt its features and structure to that that of a mobile device, then your site is due for an update. Sites that are not responsive maybe harmful to your SEO, since google prefers mobile-friendly sites.

Offsite optimization

Backlinks refer to the number of sites linking to your page; this is also a determinant factor in SEO on your site ranking in search engines. Backlinks can serve as a boost to your site, making them rank higher in search results. Google considers a backlink as a vote in your favor or a confirmation of the uniqueness and popularity of your site.

Some of the ways you can use to get more backlinks for your site include publishing articles on other blogs, allowing bloggers write a review about your product, and also by publishing sponsored posts.

It is important to check the quality of the content on your site to know if it's actually worth linking to. This may involve creating captivating well- composed and written blog post that provides relevant information to your target audience. Or creating resources relevant to your niche.

Below are strategic guidelines to getting backlinks to your sites

The first strategy we will be dealing with involves discovering where your competitors get their backlinks and find ways of getting links from the same site. Getting a backlink can be either through a resource list, product review and also when a site has a link to one of our competitors, they may also assist you by giving you a backlink to your competitor's site. You can also try to identify sites that has links to your competitor's site and then start looking out for ways to set up something that would need a backlink

1) Draft out a list of your competitors. In your list, include different brands at their various stages of growth different brand.

Ranging from well- established brands to starters that sell same products as you sell

2) Enter the URL of the competing sites one after the other into the Open Site Explorer.

3) A list of your competitor's backlinks will be displayed by the Open Site Explorer. Click on the filter drop downs and change "Link Type" to "Link equity" and "target" should be changed to "this root domain".

4) The click the request CSV Open Site Explorer button for the Open Site Explorer to send an email containing a download link to download the backlinks of your competitors.

5) The above steps should be done for all of your competitors the, then create a big Excel file where you can paste the content of CSV so you can have all of them in one file

6) Use Domain Authority to sort your data from largest to smallest. Sites with a DA greater than 70 and less than 10 are not relevant too your site because site with DA greater than 60 will be difficult and much more expensive to get back links from while sites with DA less than 10 will do little or nothing to optimize our site. So it just better to deal with DA that are not too large and not too small.

7) Here you are with a list of backlinks similar to that of your competitors. Clicking on any URL in the spreadsheet can be used to determine the page where the backlink is located.

Your competitor's link can serve as a guideline to sites that will most likely give you a link and the type of link you would likely get. You can start out with them using their contact form. Offering suggestions such as product reviews, placing a guest article on the site of interest is not a bad idea.

The other method of generating backlinks to your site is by figuring out broken links from other sites and linking them your site. Broken links are links which have an open end because the page they were initially linked to are missing on the server. Broken links affect the SEO of a site and can cause setbacks for a site. Website owners count it as a favor to be shown that they have broken links. What you have to do is to look for sites that have broken links which were formerly connected to site like yours. If you get one, try contacting the owner to inform about the website broken link after which you suggest that your site is available for him to link up with. That's a way of getting back links without going through the OSE.

Back link tips to consider:

a. Backlinks should not only be linked to your homepage, you can also have back links for other of your pages such as products, pages, collections, and blog posts.

b. Do not use one message text or link call to action for all your links. Use several text like your brand name, "see more", "click here" and in some cases, the anchor text may be a primary keyword.

c. Dedicate time weekly to working on improving your backlink over time. Put effort to increase the number of backlinks connected to your site. Working once and for all won't produce a good result in SEO as well as backline findings. With time as your backlinks increase, your position in search results will also increase and then you will have a lesser job

d. The same way we used OSE to check the backlinks linked to your competitors is the same way you can plug in your sit and discover the backlinks connected to your site and manage the links coming in.

e. We have come a long way talking about SEO; it's time for you to optimize your online store.

Chapter 4

DROPSHIPPING

Dropshipping describes a method of ecommerce that doesn't require you having an inventory or stocking the products you sell. This way you have ordered goods delivered straight to the customer without having to see the customer. It is simply acting the middleman in business transactions you do not need to see the products you are selling. Most people on Shopify use this model for their businesses.

Advantages of Dropshipping

Little or No Capital: Dropshipping is not capital intensive, and this sounds like its biggest benefit. It means you don't have to do a lot of saving and investment in inventory upfront. Interestingly, you only purchase a product after a customer has made payment so why bother about the capital. With the money you have, you are good to go get your dollars from dropshipping on shopify.

Starting out is Easy: You have no concerns about a warehouse for storing goods, constantly managing a warehouse, ordering goods and taking inventory simply because you do not have to deal with physical products while running your business.

The cost of inventory and managing a warehouse has been ruled out, so your expenses will be quite low when compared to the traditional retail business dealing with physical products. You can easily work from anywhere comfortable for you with all your information on your laptop such that you can manage every area of your business properly.

Wide Selection of Products: You can have a wide range of products to offer your potential customers using the dropshipping model. You add products to your store directly from suppliers stock for little or no cost. Pre-purchasing items limit the amount and variety that can be bought for display.

Easy to Scale: with dropshipping the suppliers do the bulk of the work. As sales growth increases you have less incremental work of ordering from the suppliers while they do the packaging and shipping. You can see that you can grow your business with dropshipping while undergoing less pains.

Does dropshipping look appealing, right? Yes to both startups and already established merchants. However, it has its own drawback which can be well managed for good results.

Disadvantages

Low Margins: The ease of starting a business with dropshipping has made a lot of people delve into it with little or no concerns about profit margins. Most competitive niche experience this low margins because items are sold for very low prices solely with the aim of generating revenue and more traffic to their site. No matter how untrusted these merchants people will look forward to checking for the price difference in the two products, their authenticity and may end up patronizing which will further reduce the profit margins.

Shipping Complexities:

Most dropshippers have several suppliers in charge of supplying their products. The shipping rate of goods will vary depending on the location of the supplier. This variation in shipping rate might seem uncalled for to a potential customer because he is ordering products from one website and to just one location. Why then should it vary?

Supplier Error: Some suppliers offer low quality packaging, delay delivery, and sometimes supply wrong products. All these would be blamed on you and may harm your business reputations, and you have to take responsibility for the errors.

As earlier said in this book, Shopify permits you to use dropshipping to grow your business, now you more about dropshipping you might want to focus more on its advantages while you carefully avoid its disadvantages.

Chapter 5

WHY USE SHOPIFY?

On a normal day, starting an ecommerce business goes with a lot of stress. You would need to select and register a business name, select and search for a suitable website name to go with the company name, work differently from your physical store and try to combine the two, and eventually start building an online presence

Shopify has done great work in making everything available, payment gateways, hosting, a web domain, a theme of your choice, the list goes on and on. It is not all out to make money from empty promises while it offers nothing. Many businesses have succeeded in the online world by using Shopify, and I can assure you that your best bet for ecommerce is Shopify.

If you still feel a sense of doubt, you may want to consider renowned companies like Wikipedia, Pixar, and Evernote which use Shopify for their only stores. Over time Shopify has proven beyond doubt to be secure, reliable and trusted.

Waste no more time, go ahead and gain more profit and popularity by using Shopify, the trusted ecommerce center!

Conclusion

Thank you again for purchasing this book!

I hope this book was able to help you to see Shopify in a true and better light.

The next step is to hurry now and create a store on Shopify.

Finally, if you enjoyed this book, then I'd like to ask you for a favor, would you be kind enough to leave a review for this book? It'd be greatly appreciated!

Thank you and good luck!